HERAKLES

HER

AKLES

a play in verse by ARCHIBALD MacLEISH

1967: HOUGHTON MIFFLIN COMPANY BOSTON

First printing   w

An earlier version of this play directed by Alan Schneider
with Rosemary Harris as Megara was produced by the Artists'
Producing Association in November 1965.

For George Seferis

AUTHOR'S NOTE

As the generation of Euripides knew the myth, it was after the Labors had been accomplished and the dog dragged from the gate of death that Herakles, unknowing, killed his sons.

HERAKLES

CHARACTERS: Herakles
Professor Hoadley
Hotel Manager
Guide

Megara
Mrs. Hoadley
Miss Parfit
Little Hodd

Xenoclea
Xenoclea as Apollo

Hotel porters
Waiter

TIME: Now

PLACE: Greece — a Grand Hotel in Athens
and a ruined temple on a hilltop

ACT ONE

Drawing-room of a high-ceilinged elegant hotel suite: long, curtained French windows across the back; entrance door stage right; bedroom door stage left; blazing crystal chandelier. A man's voice off; a not quite English English. Then, backing and bowing through the entrance door, the short black coat and striped pants of the hotel manager.

The Manager: An honor, a distinguished honor, a quite ineffably distinguished honor . . .

and not for me alone or for the house, the management . . . for Athens . . .

for all Greece . . .

In the door a pair of polished shoes on the shining foot-rest of a wheel-chair, sharply pressed trousers over wasted legs.

the great, the world-renowned professor, the famed scientist, fresh from his beneficent discoveries,

1

his Prize at Stockholm, his magnificent, incom-
    parable
ever to be treasured, towering speech . . .

He stops, blocking the progress of the chair.

We heard it even here in Hellas —
what celebration of this gallant time,
this glorious century! What scorn for
whimpering desperation in an age like this!

Posture

"Our hands full of triumph: our mouths full
    of . . ."

Hoadley: (*Off*) *a full, vibrant, sanguine voice*

                    Ha!

The Manager: *above himself*

"Our hands full of triumph!"
                             Oh, not his!
Not his! Humanity's, he meant. Our generation,
conquerors of pestilence and space.

"Our hands full of triumph and our mouths . . ."
                               Forgive me!

*The wheel-chair lunges forward, The Manager retreats, Hoadley
appears, a huge bulk of a man, strong hands straining at the
flanges of the wheels.*

2

And at the end that sounding summary:
"Age of scientific glory,
years of snivelling despair!"

Hoadley: Good, wasn't it?

The Manager: His excellency will forgive me —
No. It was not good. It was magnificent.
Unborn children will repeat it . . .

He retreats again, nudged by the chair.

                               Marvellous!

Behind Hoadley is his wife, a handsome, haunted woman in her thirties; his daughter, Little Hodd, a spoiled girl of thirteen or so; Little Hodd's governess, Miss Parfit, obviously British, obviously spinster; two overloaded porters; a waiter with a silver bucket of champagne on one hand and a silver tray of hotel fruit on the other. But The Manager is not through. He holds them herded in the entrance.

Not the glory: even Rome was glorious.
Not the snivelling despair:
he spat on snivelling despair.
But when in human history before have
triumph and despair, he said, been mated.

Hoadley: That shook them?

The Manager: Oh, that shook them, Excellency.
"Voyages among the galaxies and boys . . ."

3

how did he say it? . . .
"tresses . . ."
"with girls' tresses . . ."

apologetic titter

Mrs. Hoadley: Would it be quite convenient if we left the
rest of our magnificent oration
just till we see our rooms?

Hoadley: *Grinning up at her*

"Discoveries
never imagined by mankind . . ."

The Manager: *completing the quotation with enthusiasm*

". . . and children
fornicating out of boredom:
sodomy for something bold to do!"

*He chokes with enthusiasm. Hoadley jerks the
wheel-chair forward, whirls it staring round the
room. The laugh breaks off.*

I know . . .
Forgive me, Herr Professor.
Your Excellency's gracious cable . . .

Hoadley: I specified two double rooms . . .

The Manager: . . . modest in price and moderate in location —
I know. But with that name, that signature . . .
the most illustrious signature in science . . .

4

what could I do? What else was . . . suitable?

Hoadley: Two
                    reasonable
                            double
                                    rooms!

The Manager: But these are reasonable: they cost nothing —
                    what you
                wish. Did not the great Professor
                offer his tribute to this land in Stockholm?
                Did he not say of Greece what only
                generosity perceives and says —
                that here, still here, in this small country
                beached by the westward wind of time
                like some ship's bottom on a broken shore,
                is man's first, last, eternal patria,
                the fatherland of his heroic soul?

                He darts across to the French windows.

                Look, distinguished Excellency! Turn your
                chair . . .
                        No, this way, this way . . .
                                            Now!

                He pulls the curtains open. Black, blank glass.
                Switches off the chandelier. In the blankness,
                pulsing from rose to gold, the small, far image
                of the temple of Athena on its acropolis.

Miss Parfit: *shrilling with excitement*

                Son et lumière! In Athens!

5

Mrs. Hoadley: Think of it! The Acropolis in lights!

The Manager: The Acropolis!

Mrs. Hoadley: Exquisite dilapidation . . .
                       Like all the rest of Greece . . .
                                             that radiant
                       smile, that marble certainty, that
                       smirk!

The Manager: Every evening you can see it!
                       Every evening! And from this one room!

Mrs. Hoadley: Charming! And could we now just . . . *see?*

The Manager: *hurt*

                       Forgive me!

                       he reaches for the switch.

Hoadley: *stopping him with a gesture*

                                   Aegeus, on that very cliff . . .

The Manager: The sail upon the distant water . . .

Hoadley: The old man watching for the distant sail,
                       White or black. White if the returning . . .

The Manager: Red, your Excellency. If the hero
                       conquered and returned, a red sail:
                       black if the labyrinth . . .

6

Hoadley:	And saw the ship shadow the water, the black sail . . .
Miss Parfit:	Pure inadvertence. Theseus had forgotten. You remember Theseus, Little. He'd forced the labyrinth and killed the bull and saved the maidens and forgotten —
The Manager:	. . . raised the black forgetful sail.
Mrs. Hoadley:	Heroes are like that, darling: they forget the little things . . . like sails.
Miss Parfit:	And old Aegeus saw it . . .
Hoadley:	. . . shrieked and from the cliff Acropolis fell shrieking down.
Miss Parfit:	They named the water for him. The Aegean.
Hoadley:	Oh they were wonderful, those old Greeks! Think of imagining that mortal figure face to face with the incalculable beastliness, the man-mouthed bull . . . in ignorance . . . at night . . .
Mrs. Hoadley:	Childish imagination, wasn't it? — fancying there was something he could do!
Hoadley:	*Childish!*

Mrs. Hoadley: Yes, that innocent
                 optimism of the ancient mind:
                 all you needed was a hero's heart
                 and even horror in the night stopped nagging . . .

Hoadley: Well, it's all come out now, hasn't it? —
                 men in their mortality like roaches
                 cracked by a cart-wheel in a rut: like house-flies
                 strangling in the spider's spittle;
                 buzzing a little and then still.

Mrs. Hoadley: At least we
                 don't deceive ourselves with stories, do we? —
                 old, worn, witless, foolish tales,
                 heroic fantasies. With us the heroes
                 hang themselves or drink or drug
                 or stifle in the River Seine . . .

                 She stumbles against a chair.

                                          Could there be
                 light?

The Manager: *stiffly*

                 I beg your pardon . . .

Hoadley: Theseus!
                 Theseus from the labyrinth retrieved . . .

                 the room beyond the room beyond the
                 last impossible unentered room
                 where no man till that night had ventured . . .

8

why should Theseus have remembered the black
   sail?
He had the minotaur to think of:
that terrible victory beyond the reach
of men or of men's minds with only
one thin, ravelling thread to lead him . . .

Mrs. Hoadley: Please! I asked you for the *lights!*

The Manager: Immediately!

*The chandelier blazes up releasing them all: Miss Parfit toward
the bedrooms with the porters at her heels; the waiter to deposit
his two burdens and withdraw; Little Hodd to plump herself into
a chair with a comic book and a cud of gum and the offended
Manager to bow and go.*

With your permission, Madam.

Mrs. Hoadley: *My*
permission!

She crosses to the bucket of champagne, fiddles
with the cork.

               What a creature! "Only from
This one room you see it." This . . . one . . .
What does he think we came to Greece for?

She has the cork out.

But that's the question, isn't it? Why did we?

Filling a glass

9

To hear your great, magnificent, incompa-
rable . . . ?

Hoadley: Please!

Mrs. Hoadley: . . . ever to be treasured . . .

imitating

"Our hands full of triumph: our mouths full
of . . ."

*She gulps the glass as though she were rinsing
her throat.*

Agh!

*Hoadley twists his chair around, watches her fill her glass again,
glances at Little Hodd deep in her comics and her gum.*

What could it mean to *him*, that . . . rhetoric!

Hoadley: What it means to the rest of us, probably.

Mrs. Hoadley: *her voice rising*

The *rest* of us!

Hoadley: Me, then.

Mrs. Hoadley: It wasn't said to the rest of us.

lifting her glass in a toast

10

It was said to the King of Sweden . . .

drinks

                                        In a public
speech . . .

drinks

                    On television . . .

drinks

                                        On the radio . . .

drinks

                                                The
        newspapers.

A raking laugh. Miss Parfit appears in the door, beckons. Little Hodd glances at her mother, goes out. Mrs. Hoadley is chanting like a child.

                    And what did it mean to the King of Sweden?
                    What did it mean to the King of Sweden?

                    She fills her glass again, turns on Hoadley.

                    Well, what *did* it mean, Professor?
                    The greatest scientist the world has heard
                        of,
                    laureate of its most exalted prize,
                    confessing at the fabulous moment of his
                        triumph,
                    his and history's, the world's . . .

Hoadley: *Confessing!*

Mrs. Hoadley: *softly*

> ... the moment of my greatest happiness for
> you ...

Hoadley: Confession is an intimate nakedness
practised by women for their priests. It wasn't
me that spoke there.

Mrs. Hoadley: *her laugh*

> Who? Mankind?

Hoadley: *shrug*

> Somehow, at a time like that, you get to
> sounding ...

Mrs. Hoadley: Oh it wasn't God.
He's dead now, isn't he?
    Odd he should be dead just
now when his absence is everywhere.

Hoadley: I wasn't
there to answer for myself. They wanted
work — a man at work — a scientist
caught at being scientist — a discoverer
fresh from his discovery, his new found
land.
  When the discoverers come home
no one asks them who they are:
it's where they've been that matters — what
continents, what islands, seas ...

12

Magellan
known forever by that narrow water.
That's how they'll remember me —
not Hoadley but his voyage. That's what I
spoke for — for the voyage ...

twisting his chair to look at the pulsing image in the glass

                        this generation
struggling in the labyrinth like all the rest
before it in the history of mankind,
and suddenly, unlike the rest, compelling
passage and accomplishing the dark ...

only to bear the black sail home ...

conquering our ignorance and ending
heart-sick in the triumph of ourselves!

We should be gods to know what we know.

Mrs. Hoadley: Aren't we? I thought we were!

Hoadley: A god
can bear to know. We can't.

Mrs. Hoadley: *back at the champagne bucket*

                        And that's his
happiness?
            Or ours?
                        Oh, I can quote too:
"Happiness? Is there happiness? Are women

sea-born on the surges of themselves?"

That was
beautiful about the sea-born women . . .
wasn't it?

And men: "Are they harmonious? —
noble in their satisfactions?"

Satisfactions!
That was splendid too — the men.

So then . . .

that left the children, didn't it?

She fills her glass carefully.

"Our children: are they beautiful and delighted?

Are their lives like
bells?"

Like bells!

That left the children.

She sips slowly.

Only you answered for the children:
"Boys with girls' tresses . . ."

The wine spills.

Well, he's not a boy:
he's seventeen.

Her voice breaking.

And they're not tresses:

14

himself must suffer with us and go shuddering
home to his eternity all wounds and woe.

Men don't live their lives in history.
They live their lives in the eternal tale,
the oldest story: the heroic,
mutinous, revolted man
who will not eat his bread in suffering,
will not get his kind in suffering . . .
will not tolerate in God the terrible,
slow, cold sloth of suffering.

Mrs. Hoadley: Will not
tolerate the suffering of his son!

Herakles! Against the *universe!*

Hoadley: Yes, against the universe — the horror
howling in the door of death,
the beastly stables, crawling monsters!
Herakles who won't put up with it,
won't give in to it, won't despair
or hope or trust or anything — who struggles —
dares to struggle — dares to overcome —
to drag the dog up from the gate of Hell,
to silence death itself, to master
everything on earth and under it!

Mrs. Hoadley: *her laugh*

Who wins the wreath. And then what happens?
What happens to the glorious hero
heaped with honors when the story ends? . . .

19

She breaks down.

Oh, what happens now, my darling?
What happens now when everything is
     mastered
everything won — acclaimed — rewarded?
What happens to him now?

Hoadley: Herakles
asked that question.

Mrs. Hoadley: And they told him?

Hoadley: No.
The oracle refused. He broke the
door down — told the answer for himself.

Mrs. Hoadley: What answer?

Hoadley: That he'd tell the answer for himself.

Mrs. Hoadley: And that's the end? That's all? He masters
everything on earth — even his
destiny? Even God?

Hoadley: What more could
any living, breathing creature
do?

Mrs. Hoadley: Oh, no! Not *more*. Not *do*.
There must be something else beyond the doing.
After the world is mastered he comes home . . .
he must come home. They meet him . . . his . . .

his sons. He has sons, hasn't he? They meet him
running. Oh, they run to meet him.

Hoadley: He gives the oracle himself. That ends it.

Mrs. Hoadley: No, no. That's not the end that ends things.
Let's go tomorrow. Let's find out.
There's always some one ruin where the story
hangs around the tumble of the stones
like yellow flowers, like the curlews.
We'll go tomorrow and we'll find the stones.
They'll tell us how the end goes in the story.
You come too.

She touches him.

            We'll find a cart
or donkeys or a horse or something.
Dear Miss Parfit will conduct:
she'll bring her best and oldest Baedeker,

Say you'll come. We'll take a cheese —
a goat-cheese — bread, a skin of wine . . .

Think how Little Hodd will chatter!
What a tale she'll have to tell . . .

sudden violence

You think it's marvellous! I think it's mad!
To want the world without the suffering is mad-
        ness!
What would we be or know or bear
or love without the suffering to love for?

21

Hoadley: To want the world without the suffering is all
             there is on earth to want and man's
             rebellious labor . . . ultimate pride.

             catching her wrist dragging her toward the window

             Look at those marble columns on their hill-top!
             No, look at them! — Our signal to the stars,
             our purest, proudest signal.
                                    And of what?
             The misery of our lives? Disgust? Self-pity?
             Terror? Sickening despair?

             Our victory over pain and pity!
             Human perfection! The triumphant mind!
             Athena!
                      Not the terrified Aegeus
             whimpering on his watchman's rock
             but man-made gold Athena in her glory —
             pure intelligence!

                              A woman's body
             burning in starlight to the stars!

Mrs. Hoadley: God
             damn you! Let me go! Your hand hurts.

*He laughs, twisting her toward the window. She throws her wine
in his face. He sits grinning up at her, the wine shining on his
face.*

22

ACT TWO

A huge closed door between the stubs of enormous columns in a high deserted place; broken steps of stone before it; drums of marble scattered in the dry, sparse grass; early morning.

Silence.

Goatbells on the wind a great way off.

A long silence.

Goatbells faintly on the wind.

Silence.

Little Hodd runs in, laughing, climbing, peering.

Little Hodd: What's *that?*

Miss Parfit: *on her heels, breathless*

What's what?

Little Hodd: That *door!*

Miss Parfit: *pulling at the guidebook in her pocket*

It's the adyton isn't it?

Little Hodd: What's the . . . ?

Mrs. Hoadley: *behind Miss Parfit*

Ah, you've found it!

Miss Parfit: *to Little Hodd*

Door to an oracle.

Little Hodd: They gave the oracles behind a *door?*

Mrs. Hoadley: The prophetess did.

Miss Parfit: Pythoness.

Mrs. Hoadley: *corrected*

Pythoness.

Little Hodd: I thought Apollo gave the oracles.

Mrs. Hoadley: Hush!

laughing

You mustn't speak his name.
Things remember in these places.

Little Hodd: I thought that — you know — gave the oracles.

Miss Parfit: *heartily*

> Apollo? But of course he did.
> The Pytho was a country woman — oldish —
> sat there on her golden tripod
> dressed in holy white like brides,
> not a wit in her head, and yet she prophesied.
> He put his voice in her mouth, a great
> god's voice like a rusty conch-shell
> raving in a gale of wind:
> she shuddered and shouted.
>   Powerful kings
> fell in a faint, they say, when she shouted.
> They knew who it was.
>   Ah . . .

turning a page of her guidebook

>   Here!
> "Ancient oracle constructed
> back before the start of time
> precisely over the crack at the center . . ."

puzzling

> ". . . precisely over the crack . . ."?
>   ". . . at the center . . ."?
> What extraordinary English!

Mrs. Hoadley: Greek more likely —
English Greek.

25

Miss Parfit: Crack at the center of
what?

Mrs. Hoadley: The universe?

Miss Parfit: Ah, yes. The
universe. Quite. But why the crack?

Mrs. Hoadley: So he could hear them, possibly.

Little Hodd: *down on her hands and knees, mouth close to the*
stones: a high clear childish voice

Halloooooooo ...

Silence: the goatbells.

So *who* could hear them?

Mrs. Hoadley: The god.

Little Hodd jumps to her feet eyeing the stones.

At home
nobody knows if he can hear:
we ask just the same. Oh, we ask!

Miss Parfit: *still at her book*

Ah, there's more: it's connected with Herakles.

Mrs. Hoadley: I know.

Miss Parfit: You *know?*

26

Mrs. Hoadley: I mean they told me.

Little Hodd: Hercules?

Miss Parfit: Not in the least. The Greek one.
                Herakles.

Mrs. Hoadley: Hercules was Roman, darling.
                A sort of strong boy in the cinema.

Little Hodd: In *Rome?*

Mrs. Hoadley: Anyway the Romans thought of him:
                oversize like everything they thought of.
                Herakles was quite, quite different —
                Grrreeek!

                to herself, a little laugh

                Man against the universe.

Miss Parfit: *matter-of-fact*

                Precisely. Man against the universe.

Little Hodd: But he's the *one.* I know. Don't tell me.
                He's the one who cleaned the stables.
                Didn't he clean the beastly stables?

Mrs. Hoadley: Didn't he just!

Little Hodd: Fetch the apples?

Miss Parfit: *Golden* apples.

Little Hodd: Golden apples.
Somebody stole the golden apples.
Herakles fetched them.

Miss Parfit: And from *where?*

Little Hodd: *her lesson by rote*

Hesperides-those-westward-islands . . .

And that wasn't all. He killed the monsters —
hundred-headed hydras . . .

Miss Parfit: Lions.

Little Hodd: Man-eating mares . . .

She can't go on.

Miss Parfit: And *then* what happened?

No response.

Then what happened?

Little Hodd: I don't know.

Mrs. Hoadley: Nobody knows, my baby.

Miss Parfit: Oh, but they
do! It's the end of the story.

Mrs. Hoadley: Possibly

                    no one gets to the end of the story ...
                    or no one has. Not yet.

Miss Parfit: What *do* you
                    mean, not yet? It's in the mythologies.

Mrs. Hoadley: Is it? Why then so are we.

                    a laugh

                    That's what Professor Hoadley tells me ...

                    He wanted to come.

Miss Parfit: *Here? This mountain?*

Little Hodd: *peering off*

                    Look!

Miss Parfit: Where?

Mrs. Hoadley: It's just a guide.
                    They always find you in the end. Like vultures.

Little Hodd: But everyone says they're *Communists!*

Miss Parfit: Most of them
                    back in the mountains here, I dare say.
                    Anyway they don't like *us.*

Little Hodd: But what will he
                    do?

                                29

Mrs. Hoadley: Guide.

Miss Parfit: Tell us history
                    nobody knows and nobody ought to.

Little Hodd: I don't like it.

Mrs. Hoadley: Just be busy
                    looking or having thoughts or something.

Little Hodd: Thoughts about *what?*

*The Guide comes up over the edge of things: official cap, patched
coat, ingratiating manner, sardonic eye.*

The Guide: Munificent travellers!

*Miss Parfit makes an elaborate business of picking around in the
rubble with Little Hodd under her lee. Mrs. Hoadley contem-
plates the enormous door.*

                    I trust the climb was not too tiring:
                    mountains are sometimes rather steep . . .

stalking Miss Parfit

                    sometimes more than others . . .

a pounce to head her off

                                        especially!

She is cornered.

30

So!
Very well!
Good morning!

a bow to Mrs. Hoadley

Good
morning!

If you call it morning:
sun up: coffee down ...

No response: pause.

If, that is, you've had your coffee ...

No response: pause: new start.

Think what it was, this famous city,

gesture off and down

town of the Immortal Tale!
And how many bars in the place now?
Two?

No response.

Three?

Nothing.

Yet *you* have come to it,
well-born, bountiful, beguiling ladies
bred a thousand miles away!

31

a bow

What am I saying! Ten thousand!

an obeisance

Miss Parfit: Thank you so very much, we haven't
come though, actually.

Mrs. Hoadley: We mean we're going.

The Guide: But of course you've come, illustrious travellers.
You've heard the story of these famous stones.
Everyone on earth has heard it:

racing up the broken steps

                                        returning
hero at the silent door
who asks and is not answered . . .

posture

                                   and still stands
unanswered . . .

raising his arm: professional theatrics

                    till the moment comes . . .

higher

the moment comes . . .

32

>   *still higher*
>
>   the ultimate moment
>
>   comes . . .

Mrs. Hoadley: . . . and he gives his oracle himself.

The Guide: *deflated, his arm falling, his fist knocking weakly
            on the enormous door. He turns to descend but
            the knock echoes once and again and again and
            again and faster and fainter and fading and gone as
            though some endless corridor had received it. Half
            terrified, half triumphant, he listens; turns on Mrs.
            Hoadley.*

>   Precisely! As the erudite, enlightened
>   lady tells us in her elegant words,
>   he gives his oracle himself. Even the
>   dumb, reverberating bronze remembers it.

>   *back up the steps*

>   Here within this door the hero,
>   Herakles, his deeds accomplished,
>   his destiny denied him by the god,
>   pitches the Pytho from her golden chair and . . .

bow to Mrs. Hoadley

>   tells his oracle himself!

*He taps the door with his finger; the echo as before, once
and again and again and again and faster and fainter and
fading.*

Little Hodd: *clutching Miss Parfit*

It's *true!*

Miss Parfit: It isn't true. It's in the story.

Little Hodd: I mean it *was* true *once.*

Miss Parfit: That's history!
In history everything *was* true *once* —
such a comfort! In the story
nothing was ever true at all:
not once, not ever.

Mrs. Hoadley: *to herself*

Only always.

Little Hodd: What did you
say?

Mrs. Hoadley: I said ...

She laughs.

I said, in the story
nothing was ever true once: only always.

Your father told me that. He told me
all our lives are in the story ...

Little Hodd: Yes, oh *yes!* We're in the story —
Where shall we start?

34

Miss Parfit: I *must* say . . .

The Guide: *gestures toward the steps*

                                                    So!

Little Hodd seats herself.

                              Our little conference!

Mrs. Hoadley takes her place.

                                        The famous story! . . .

Mrs. Hoadley: If he'll tell how it ends.

Miss Parfit: *If* he knows!

Little Hodd: *a child's sing-song*

                    I know! I know!
                    I know where we are . . .

          Down on her hands and knees acting it out

                                        the monsters!

Mrs. Hoadley: Oh, we must be past the monsters.
                    Nobody's seen a monster, not for . . .
                    years.

Miss Parfit: If ever!

Mrs. Hoadley: Ah, they heard them . . .

munching in the chinks of wind,
the hesitations of the rain, the silence
after the one word said, the other
never said . . .

                    never spoken.

Miss Parfit: Mrs. Hoadley, dear, what is it?
What's come over you?

Mrs. Hoadley: Why . . .

                                    nothing . . .
nothing at all.

She laughs.

                We're past the monsters.

Little Hodd: No, begin at the beginning.
It has to begin. He's born, isn't he?

The Guide: *launched*

           Precisely. The hero, Herakles, is born . . .

Little Hodd: Strangles serpents in his cradle.

The Guide: Strangles serpents in his cradle . . .

Little Hodd: Smooth, thick, silken serpents!

Miss Parfit: *Please!*

The Guide: Perhaps the young and studious scholar . . .

Little Hodd: Afterward he grows and grows
and grows right up and he's a hero.

The Guide shrugs.

    Isn't he?

The Guide: If you say so, Miss . . .

    nastily

    Forty-nine sons in a single night
on forty-nine of the daughters of . . .

Little Hodd: . . . somebody,
the fiftieth declining as unworthy of the honor.

Miss Parfit: *Little Hoadley!* You know *that?*

The Guide: Of course she knows it. Every school-girl . . .

Miss Parfit: Not quite every school-girl, thank you!

Little Hodd: And after that he marries . . .

The Guide: *sourly*

                Megara.
Little Hodd: Megara.

Mrs. Hoadley: Megara, the Prince's daughter:
rope of braided gold her hair,
heart all hope, all hope.

Little Hodd: And she has
                            seven sons . . .

                    puzzling

                                and then what happens?

The Guide: *giving up: rattling it off*

                    He undertakes the impossible labors
                    shags the monsters shovels the dung
                    accomplishes everything returns . . .

                    gesture over his shoulder toward the door

Little Hodd: *on her feet, tapping and toeing as though she were
                    marking time to a tune in her head*

                    And *that's* where we are in the story, story:
                    past the daughters . . .

Mrs. Hoadley: *on her feet, her mocking laughter*

                                        Rustle of feathery
                    soft leaves in the thicket and one of them
                    down in a heap and the rest running or
                    not quite running . . .

Miss Parfit: *Mrs.* Hoadley!

Little Hodd: *circling her mother, laughing, spinning*

                    Rustle of feathery soft leaves in the . . .

                                38

Miss Parfit: Oh, *please* stop it!

Mrs. Hoadley: Ferns to fall in:
                 glint of silver in the crumpled ferns . . .

Miss Parfit: Little Hoadley! Will you *stop!*

Little Hodd: No! Oh, no! Oh, no! Go on!
                 Go on where he marries the maiden, the Megara.

Mrs. Hoadley: *suddenly still*

                 The maiden . . .
                            the maiden . . .
                                       the maiden . . .
                                              the Megara . . .

                 Bride-bed in the smoky glare,
                 the golden pair, the lurching torches . . .

Little Hodd: *whirling, laughing*

                 The golden pair, the lurching torches . . .

Mrs. Hoadley: Roses . . .
                            the recurring song,
                 recurring song,
                            recurring song . . .

                 she turns away

                 The several roses . . .
                            the recurring song . . .

39

Little Hodd: *stumbling*

> I can't see those lurching torches.

Miss Parfit: *a sniff*

> Nor anyone else that marries in churches.

Little Hodd: Mother! What are you doing, mother?

Mrs. Hoadley: *fumbling in her purse, to The Guide*

> Thank you so very much, we must be . . .

The Guide: But of course. Your many duties call you —
all those journeys still to take,
the waiting world . . .

> *sardonic bow, cap in hand open side up*

> I trust our little
inconclusive conversation . . .

Sudden violence, knocking the proffered coins from her fingers with a slap of his cap.

> You will not understand it, will you? —
you and all the rest of you, your likes, your
tittering kind! You think the story
tells itself forever like a bird-song
over and over and will never end
as long as there are fools to listen. Well, it
ends! It ends, deluded travellers! —
Now, in our own time, it's ended!

working himself into a frenzy of eloquence

    Impossible labors in the muck accomplished —
    undertakings in the ordure and the blood —
    the world won, the monsters mastered,
    death without the dog and all
    the golden apples plucked to eat!
                         To
    eat, presumptuous visitors, and not by
    you. Not *you!*

  gesture toward the blue behind him

        The victorious hero
    mounts already the forbidden road,
    runs to the dreadful door . . .

*Megara appears among the stones, a fine woman in the full of
life, shawl fallen back from golden hair. The Guide breaks off,
resumes his professional manner.*

                        I beg your
    pardon, Madam!

She pays no attention, moves toward the steps.

                       I *beg* your pardon!

*She finds a place to sit, pulls a little clutch of mending from
under her shawl.*

    You will have to go back to the gate and come
    in by the . . .

She threads her needle.

                    I said . . .

Little Hodd: *staring at Megara*

                    Look! . . .

Miss Parfit: Don't encourage her.

Little Hodd: What do you mean, don't encourage her:
she isn't begging.

Miss Parfit: Oh, my child!
Sitting around like that on a . . .
                  monument!

Little Hodd: She *isn't!* Beggars never sew.

Miss Parfit: Who taught you that?

Mrs. Hoadley: She sews beautifully —
like a well-bred girl from a good house
where daughters learn from mothers.

Miss Parfit: Oh,
they learn for themselves, a girl's hands.
Think what they know for themselves without a
soul to tell them . . .

Megara: *looking up from her sewing*

              Is this where he comes?

She looks from one to the other, nods.

It is, isn't it?
                    Or you wouldn't be here . . .
        not this time of morning anyway . . .

She sews for a while, bites off the thread.

        You'd think I'd be the first to know . . .
        I never have been . . .
                            Even Tirida.

"Wasn't he wonderful at Tirida?"

She laughs: a lovely lilting laugh like a young girl's.

        I'd never even heard of Tirida!

"Wonderful!" I said.

the laugh again

                        Wonderful!
        Ashamed not to, I suppose.
        I was younger then . . .

back to her stitching

                        minded more.
        Now I mind and don't mind.

A long silence while she works.

                            No, I
        mind . . .

43

I mind . . .

Silence: at last she looks up.

It *is* here, isn't it?
If, I mean, he comes at all:
someone always thinks he's seen him —
says he thinks . . .

The Guide: *sourly*

If you mean Herakles,
Where else would he come?

Megara: Almost anywhere —
home even: he has a home . . .
sons . . .

She goes back to her work.

sons he hasn't seen for
years . . .
longer . . .

The Guide: He comes here:
triumphant hero to the dreadful door.

Megara: What would he want of the dreadful door?

The Guide: His oracle.

Megara: *her lilting laugh*

He has his oracle.

44

We all have, every one of us: we'll die
but not quite yet and in between
we have the sunlight on the green a little.
warmth beside us in the bed at night,
hands that touch hands, our little, leeward
lifetime where the cold sea wind
that blows the world down will not blow —
not yet . . .
                                not quite.

The Guide: That's not the oracle
Herakles asks for, is it, ladies?
He wants the future for himself —
all the future.

Megara: *That's* the future.

The Guide: Not for him it isn't — hero!
Not with the monsters mastered and the great
world waiting like an unused day.

Megara: Who knows what's waiting in a day?

The Guide: *a jerk of his head toward the closed door*

                                The god does.

Megara: Does he? Why then ask him something.
Ask him when we'll die — that's something.

She pulls her shawl suddenly over her head.

No! No! No! Don't ask him!

45

Rising, facing the sun

> Sun, that in this stony place
> blinds the lidless eyes of stone,
> I also cannot face your face.
>
> Hide from me, Sun, what comes to pass
> beyond these moments on this grass . . .
>
> beyond this warmth against these bones.

Silence: in the silence, a great way off, a man's shout blown by the wind.

Little Hodd: Listen!

Megara: Yes! Listen! Listen!

The shout again.

> It is! It's *his* voice! Oh, I'd know it
> anywhere. I've heard him shouting
> off-shore in the raging winters
> faint as that above the surf!

The Guide: *staring at her*

> *You* have!

Megara: Often.

The cry again.

>   Listen to him
> shout!

46

She is radiant: laughing — almost crying.

He's home!
... here ...
it doesn't
matter ...
all those years and years and
never certain, never told,
never a dream at night but something
followed snuffling on a bloody scent and
screamed and I woke screaming ...

*She breaks off: the laughter suddenly gone, the relief
turned rage.*

and for
what? For what? Fabulous victories!
Slaughters never known or thought of!
Monsters dying never died before!
Triumph after triumph after
nobody knows what impossible triumphs!
Each more difficult than the last! More dan-
gerous!

throwing her mending onto the steps

Worse than dangerous! ...
dotty! ...
downright
dotty for a grown-up man!

Boys would know better!

47

Mrs. Hoadley: That's a wife!

Miss Parfit: Or a wife's tongue.

Mrs. Hoadley: Where there's one there's the other.

Megara: *stooping, picking up her things, raging still*

> And all for what?
> > All for what?
>
> Why would any grown, intelligent,
> sensible, thinking man go off,
> move out, leave his roof-tree,
> live among the monstrous shapes alone
> in the wild sky?

The Guide: Because he *does*.

> Because he's Herakles and he does. Because he
> can't put up with it, won't put up with it.
> You ought to know that much about him,
> knowing his voice on the wind.

Megara: You think

> I haven't wakened at the turn of night
> when stars and stillness ask those questions?

settling down on the steps again, threading her needle

> Oh, I knew he'd tackle something . . .
> had to . . .
> > most men have to . . .
> > > can't just
> sit and suck their lives . . .

48

Mrs. Hoadley: Some do.

Miss Parfit: *a sniff*

> Yes, some do, but they don't marry.
> Anyway don't marry *you:*
> not if you're bright!

Megara: I knew he'd tackle
> something . . .
>   but the whole, wild world! . . .

She is on her feet again.

> couplings and croupings, grapplings and groans,
> snakes coiled and horrors howling,
> centaurs with their horses' pizzles
> trampling the sheets, the screaming girls
> miscarrying a five-month later . . .
>
> nasty little naked hooves like
> thumbs!
>   No! I wasn't prepared for it.

Miss Parfit: It never occurred to you men go off?
> I mean . . .
>   just go? . . .
>   about their . . . business?

Megara: *turning on her*

> One thing *did* occur to me! It wasn't
> *that!*
>   Not what you're thinking.

49

Miss Parfit: *frightened*

But I wasn't . . .

Megara: You looked and it's worse. A woman may be
             daft by daylight in an empty house
             remembering what never happened:
             not by night — not the nights —
             not remembering what night brings back to you.

             You don't imagine those things, lady:
             not if you've known.
                              I knew.

Miss Parfit: I never . . .

Megara: *She is laughing again.*

             Of course you did.
                              It doesn't matter.
             It's true that he went: true too
             I don't know why he went . . .
                              Oh,
             I know what he said. He had a promise —
             got it from here I don't doubt:
             clean the world up, silence Hell —
             something would come of it.

Mrs. Hoadley: What would come of it?

Megara: *a long, lovely laugh — true laughter*

             He'd be a god!

50

Or like one . . .
                                You know.
That's how oracles go on:
promise you anything and when you get it
what you've got is what they promised you —
figure it out for yourself . . .
                                I never
cared for them much.

The Guide: But it's true! It's come
true! He's cleaned the world up, hasn't he?
The mortal hero with the naked hands —
he's killed the monsters, hasn't he? — silenced
Hell? If he isn't a god what is he?

Megara: You think it's *true?*

The Guide: I think it's happened.

Megara: If truth were only true because it
happened to have happened what would
truth be? Anything can happen.

Mrs. Hoadley: Even a
man turned god?

Megara: A man turned god!

        her laugh

        It's worse than a god turned gander, isn't it?

To Little Hodd.

I never was one to go swimming with swans
in the hope that our father in heaven had
        feathers.
It's enough to believe in a man's skin
and a man behind the skin to touch you.

The shout again, nearer.

        Listen to him! . . .

Again.

                On the steep now.

Turning to Miss Parfit, forgiving her.

        Maybe he did, you know . . .
                        just go —
not for promises or pride or hope or
anything but just for going.

Men are like that, aren't they? Only
happy when they're wrestling lions,
scrambling around in the dark discovering
ways up, ways on,
better, nobler lives . . .
                        It never
even seems to cross their minds
this one might be good enough to
live . . .
        or try to.
                Oh, I'd see him
evenings underneath his trees
picking stones up, looking at them,

letting them drop as a man will
sometimes when his mind is maundering . . .

I should have wondered, I suppose.
I didn't.

He'd come in, eat heartily,
sleep from light to light in the cool
room, the sea-wind in the rattling shutters,
play with his sons, the seven of them
yelping round him like so many spaniels . . .

They're grown now: great things . . .

Then one morning he was gone:
not a wave nor a word nor anything . . .
$$\text{just gone.}$$

*She sits motionless in silence, her head down. The goatbells
drift in the wind.*

Partings tear . . .
They never can be
mended if they last too long . . .

*The shouting voice suddenly nearer: a single unintelligible word.
She pulls her shawl over her head.*

Little Hodd: What did he
          say?

The Guide: *climbing among the stones: peering off*

He called Xenoclea.

53

Little Hodd: What's . . .
                      Xenoclea?

The Guide: The Pytho. In the story.
                      Back of the door there in the story.

Little Hodd: She gave the oracle?

The Guide: Or didn't give it.

Miss Parfit: It is! It *is!* It's Herakles!
                                      That's the
                      skin of the Nemean lion!

        shrill with excitement

                                      But it actually
                is!

The Guide: *scurrying off among the stones like a hare hunting
            cover*

            I told you . . .

Herakles: *lunging in: a great, battered, tattered, bearded, time-
          scarred, triumphant man*

                      God Apollo! Xenoclea!

Silence.

            Xenoclea!

54

He hesitates at the bottom step, retreats, listens: only the goat-bells.

Apollo!

Megara: *to herself, her head down over her work, her shawl concealing her face*

Trust your fingers . . .
A woman has to trust her fingers . . .

Some things they remember for themselves
the way the leaves remember rain . . .

Scar across the skin . . .
that silken
secret in the night against your fingers . . .

Herakles: *at the bottom step, respectful, cautious*

Apollo! Lord God Apollo!

Silence: he stares around him, spots The Guide.

You, there! Where's he gone to? Shut
down?
Closed up?

The Guide emerges, cringing.

And the Pythia —
where's the Pythia? She always answers.

Can't you answer either?

55

                              Look!
          I'm back. I'm home. Enemies defeated,
          deeds done, bloody, mucking
          world made over like a summer day;
          where's the welcome for it?

      gesture toward the three women

                                          That?

Bark of laughter. To Mrs. Hoadley.

          It isn't every rose-red morning
          someone stops you on a stony hill
          to say the world's made over, is it?

      smacks her on her smooth behind

Mrs. Hoadley: *flaring*

          Not every morning, no. Nor noon,
          nor night, nor sunrise either, nor the day the
          rain stops, nor the day you marry
          carrying hyacinths . . .

The Guide: I told them, Herakles.
          I told them the great tale was done,
          the stables shovelled out at last,
          heaven shouldered off at last,
          dread dragged up from Hell itself at
          last . . .

Herakles: And not an enemy . . .

                              56

The Guide: ...an enemy...

Herakles: *triumphant*

     I killed them in the gate of Thebes!
     Last night, at sundown in the gate of Thebes...

     You knew that, didn't you? You told them...

  cuffs him

     Told Apollo too I dare say...

  cuffs him

     Only he doesn't need your telling!
     He knows: he saw it...

  starting cautiously toward the steps

           He sees everything...

  up the first step

     Last night...
        at sundown...
            when the smouldering sun
    set the heaped-up sky on fire
    kindling the air...

  hesitating

        You saw it, didn't you? —
  blood-red blaze across the dying sky...

The Guide: What did he see? What happened, Herakles?

Herakles: Not what *you* think — screaming trumpets,
                roaring crowds, ascending eagles
                circling into sun, the god-thank
                spoken and the hero home . . .
                nothing like that! . . .
                                        My own city . . .

                twelve years without the sight or
                sound or smell of your own city
                starves the heart . . .
                                        and I came home to it —
                last night at sundown I came home.

                Thebes. I ask you — my own town!
                Dogs as usual. Dust as usual.
                Someone sprinkling water on the dust as
                usual . . .
                                the old, sad smell . . .
                I stood there in the dust of my own city
                breathing the night . . .
                                        and all at once
                my enemies were round me, leaping, laughing,
                big as bullocks in the blundering light.

        triumphant shout

        I killed them in the gate of Thebes!

Megara: *her head down over her work*

                Stranger . . .
                                and not by the years either:

                                58

not only the years . . .
                    I don't know . . .
like a dog come back from the wolves who's done
what dogs don't and you feel it in him . . .

et what they don't eat . . .
                              gone over . . .
killed . . .
            You don't know what he's killed!

The Guide: And that's the end of it!

Herakles: What they tell me —
               end and all and I've come home.

Megara: *to herself: softly*

               Have you, Herakles?
                         Come home?

Herakles: *a violent cry*

               Speak to me, Lord God Apollo!
               Why won't you speak to me? You know me —
               don't give out you never knew me,
               never talked to me . . .

Silence.

                              I'm Herakles!
                              You know me . . .

Little Hodd: *kneeling, her mouth close to the stones*

               He's Herakles who killed the monsters.

Herakles: Even the child has heard about it.

The Guide: They've all heard — the whole story.

Herakles: *sending him sprawling*

                Who knows the story whole?

Little Hodd: *Oh, he* does.
                He told us. All except the journey
                down below there where the dead men are.

Mrs. Hoadley: It isn't far. No farther than the window.
                One short step beyond the sill.

Megara: *softly*

                Only ... to come back is difficult.

Little Hodd: How did you go?

Herakles: *perching her on a stone*

                                By going. Just by
                going. Nowhere, even death itself,
                a man can't get to if he'll only go.
                I followed the dying down. They have their
                backs turned toward us in the dark departing.

Megara: *over her work*

                It's true. They turn their heads away.

60

Little Hodd: Where? Where do they go to, Herakles?

Herakles: Great slot in the rock at Troezen.
                Swallows nest there in the lofts of stone
                twittering in their silvery voices.
                You step into night . . .
                                     steep stair . . .

        Acting it out: enormous relish

            starless, and the way goes down,
            no sound but your sound, not a glint, a glitter,
            nothing . . .
                        and you still go down . . .
            still nothing . . .
                        then the smell of water
            stale the way a wet stone smells . . .

            dead men throng that unseen shore —
            words without breath — bat voices . . .

            then the skiff comes silent on the silent
            oar: you crowd the dead: cross over:
            fumble for footing in the shelving ooze:
            grab at eel-grass: stumble: flounder:
            listen . . .
                        no sound at all, not even
            frogs to hear by . . .
                        So you whisper . . .
                                        nothing.
            Speak . . .
                    still nothing.
                            Shout! . . .

                            61

                                        You know what
              answers when you shout?
                             A tiny
              rustle like a mess of land-crabs
              Scuttling in a trash of leaves!

Little Hodd: And you can't
              see!

Herakles: You can't see.

Little Hodd: Then the dog barks?

Herakles: That was when I took the dog —
              heard him in the dark off somewhere —
              followed the snarl — my hands found him.

The Guide: Herakles! Herakles! Throttled the dog!

Herakles: Gagged him anyway.

The Guide: Men can die now
              quietly without that horrible
              howling in the dark: just die.

Miss Parfit: *shriek*

              Just *die!*

The Guide: The way the mice do, lady —
              secretly, among the shucks, the sticks,
              the stones, without a thing to frighten them —
              only to be still and die.

Mrs. Hoadley: But when they sleep!

           Hell is where you
   waken in the night from sleep
   and men still sleep . . . still waken.

The Guide: Not to
   that sound, lady. Oh, not now, not now.
   Think of those medieval cities
   tolling with their iron bells.
   Why did they toll those bells? — to drown
   what sound? And now the bells are silent!
   Herakles has gagged the dog!

   Aie! Aie! Herakles! Herakles!

he struts and jigs to the beat of his words

   Herakles wrestled with death and won,
   man against death and the live man won,
   the dry bone humbled and lay down

Herakles falls in with him.

   Herakles rattled the king of the bones,
   knuckled his neck and cracked his stones,
   the dry bone humbled and lay down.

Little Hodd: What did you do with him, Herakles?

Herakles: The dog?

Tossing her into the air

What did I do with him? Tied him up
in the cook's slops in Eurystheus' kitchen.

The Guide: Terrible great howling dread
in the cook's slops in Eurystheus' kitchen!

Herakles: That was the lot — the Labors!

Mrs. Hoadley: *retrieving Little Hodd*

                       And high
time! You'll be a god now, won't you?

Herakles: *wheeling on her: the laughter cut short*

You know that too?

Miss Parfit: She . . .

    a gesture to Megara

                  . . . she told us.

Herakles: *to Megara*

Ha! Do I look like a god to you?

She does not look up.

                   To
any of you?
        Stinking knees
black with the muck of Hell still on them!

64

They cower. Silence. He peers up at the door, pacing back and forth below the steps.

Look at me, Lord God Apollo!

Is this the way you keep the promises
given and taken when a man goes out
against the misery of the world to master it? ...

> *one step up the stair*

... and *masters* it?

Little Hodd: *Herakles!*

Miss Parfit: *every syllable the governess*

> Be patient, Herakles!
> Everything is told in time.

The Guide: In time but not in *your* time, lady!

Herakles: *Another step*

Will you not answer me, Apollo? —
a man who's done what I've done ...
                    and come back from it.

Megara: *softly*

Have you, Herakles ... ?
                    come back?

Little Hodd: That's twice she's said it. What does she mean?

65

Mrs. Hoadley: I don't know.

Little Hodd: If it's *him?*
                                            If he stayed there
                    over the water and a shade came back,
                    a shadow?
                                    If the skiff refused him
                    coming away to the world and something
                    else came?

Megara: *touching her to comfort her as a woman will a strange*
          child

                            Oh, the dead don't come.
                    How would a dead man find his way
                    to his own door from beyond afterward,
                    all those years and years between them?

      raising her voice a little

                    Even for live men with their leather shoes
                    it's long, too long, from that dark country.

Herakles: *turning on the step, staring at her*

                    No, not long. A kind of chimney
                    channeled in the rock you come by. Stars at
                    noonday in that narrow flue.
                    I had the dog-weight on my shoulders.

Megara: *drawing Little Hodd down beside her*

                    It's only at the first the dead come . . .
                    the first few months, the year. Afterward

66

even the path is gone, the stone
mute whatever words were carved on it:
the rose beside the stone uprooted . . .

lifting her voice

How can they come when the world changes
time by time?
                    A night changes it . . .

A woman looks at a man and it changes . . .

Herakles: *a step back down*

Once in the sun my eyes dazzled.
Even the thistle in the sun was strange.

Megara: Everything's strange to the returning.

She lets Little Hodd go.

You have to be part of it day by day,
night after night or even your
bed's strange . . .
                    your garments . . .

Herakles: Who
            are you?
                    Look at me!

She lets the shawl fall back from her golden head.

                    Megara!

Megara: I heard you.
            Last night in the street I heard you.

They stand staring at each other.

            Why did you think I wouldn't hear you?
            . . . wouldn't know you? . . .
                        . . . how your left foot falls
            lighter a little on the heel as though it
            ran to something?

Herakles: Megara! Megara!

Megara: You passed the door last night.

Herakles: There was no
            light, no sign, no sound.

Megara: I wanted
            them to light you: that was *their* part.

            Only your sons, they said, should welcome you.
            Day or night, they used to tell me —
            night or day when you came home,
            whenever that was, they'd be waiting.
            They'd see you long before I'd see you . . .
            that's what they said.
                            And so I let them.
            Light him in yourselves, I said.

            she shrugs

            God knows where a boy goes off to!

68

Herakles: No one else was there to open?

Megara: Oh, Herakles!

    a little rueful laugh

                  I know. I know.
There's no fool like an old fool, is there?
I thought you meant to have surprised me —
waked me from the first light sleep —
and so I lay quite still, quite still . . .

It was my pounding heart drew nearer
step by step . . .
              and never came.

Herakles: And yet I heard you. I remember
someone running to the door —
someone at the door not running.

It may be I've imagined it so long it
seems remembered.

Megara: *in his arms*

                  You went by.

Herakles: Came here.

Megara: I know — came here!
                  I always
told myself when this was over —
whenever this was over — we'd go down,

69

live on that half-acre by the sea and watch the
boys grow . . .
Sit there in the evenings watching.

It's a good time in a long day,
evening is — sun-warm door stone,
wife and husband in the dusk together
waiting a little, listening . . .
lying
knee between knees at night and listening
first for their sons and then the sea . . .

She kisses him.

Hurt heals. That's what the sea says.
Well, who knows? It still could happen.

her lilt of laughter

And that's what the sea says too. "Who knows."

Herakles: I had to come here: you know that.

Megara: Do I?

pushing him away

I suppose I do:
I suppose you've always had to!

That's why you left us, wasn't it? You *had* to! —
had to go off, go out, go wandering —
leave your fig trees to the rainy wind,

70

your roof to winter, your warm bed . . .
leave everything!
                  And why?
                             Because you
had to!
           God knows why!

Herakles:
                           He must.
He put the burden on me.

Megara:
                           Did he?

Herakles: Didn't he? Why did I go?

Megara:
                           Oh,
to set the world right, sweep the cow sheds,
track the hind no hound had scented,
hunt the beast no hurt could harm,
run him down, run them all down —
tackle every last, impossible,
unknown labor on the lovely earth . . .

Herakles: Be reasonable, woman! Unless some god had
sent him would a man go off?
                         Would he?
Live a life like that one? Live
alone?
        Alone?
              You understand that?
No encounter but the wind's encounter?

It was always like that in the world there:
shapes along the edge of light —

71

you never could tell what they were . . .
                              Clouds?
They could have been clouds . . .
                    or a hundred-headed
something slobbering in a bog . . .
                         or the sea
beasts along the sea-drowned ledges
watching with their women's eyes,
there and not there in the tumbling surges.
It was always like that — not a sign to go by,
track to go by, trace before you,
foot before you on the smooth of sand,
or a man's mark on a tree or a broken
oar or anything a man lets fall,
or a voice in the air but bird voices . . .
never a man's as a man calls
frightening crows, commanding horses . . .

a woman's that her children come to . . .

all that drifting human haze of
sound the sun lifts in the peopled countries
smelling of smoke and the night quiets it.

Would I have gone without the will of
god to send me? Or his oracle?

The Guide: Surely you understand that, lady!
              Nothing becomes of us that time
              has not intended.

Megara: As the wave intends the
              drowned man!

It isn't destiny that sends us.
Destiny's the raven in the oak
that roosts above the future when we get to it.

Destiny waits for us. We go ourselves.

Herakles: It was the god himself, I tell you:
              I had his promise.

Megara: You had mine.
              I know what mine was — be a woman to you.
              What was his?
                        The sky?

  her lilting laugh

                              Oh, the
              sky!
                  You shouldered it, didn't you?
                              They told me . . .

              And there were other tales they told . . .
              You've always friends to tell you those things.
              It didn't matter: you'd come home
              and no more said about it . . .
                              Hyperboreans:
              milk-skinned women under the frost . . .

              and the African girls in the blue shadows,
              musk and sweet as smoky plums . . .

              and whatever they're like to the west, the Hes-
                  perides —

                        73

gilded with the sun they must be:
golden sunsets over seas . . .

It didn't matter.
                    You'd come home . . .

And then you did come home —
                              and didn't.

Herakles: Great Light in the Sky! Will you listen to
              that!
                    I ask you! Will you listen!
              I do what no man's done, destroy the
              skulkers in the rubble of the dark,
              drive the birds off, those obscene, Stymphalian
              dribblers on the leaves of sleep,
              venture to death's last door, return and
              that's the music!

Megara: But it's true —
              true I mean it didn't matter.
              I had the house swept clean, the sheets
              rinsing in the wind all morning,
              lavender to bind the broom,
              bread made, water drawn . . .

              I waited till the moon went down
              and then, asleep, still waited.

Herakles: Megara!
              Listen, Megara!
                         No, but listen!
              A man who's done what I've done can't just

quit, go home, pull the door shut,
take the woman he has wanted
night after night, the more the farther,
kiss his sleeping sons and sleep.

Megara: Why?

Herakles: He needs to know, be sure.

Megara: Of what? Of *her*?

Mrs. Hoadley: For shame, Herakles!
Think of the nights she's slept without a
man against her breast for you!

Herakles: Of what he's done! Of what he's done! —
the beasts dead, the enemies around me
whistling in the gate of Thebes —
shouting my name at me.

Megara: *freezing*

                                    Your name!

Herakles: Is that the way a god comes home —
howled at in the streets?

Megara: They knew your
name . . . !

Herakles: *lunging up the steps*

                        Answer me, Xenoclea!

Silence.

What must I do, Xenoclea, to be answered?

Silence.

There's nowhere left I haven't gone to,
deed I haven't done . . .

Silence.

What must I
do?

He strikes the door with his closed fist, a great crash of sound, answered by echo after echo after echo, as before, each one louder than the last, then faster, fainter, fading.

Megara: Oh leave the oracle to the oracle.
We have our life: there's enough of it, isn't
    there,
taking it year by year as it comes . . . ?

taking a day at a time as it comes to us . . . ?

night at a time . . . ?
There's enough in a man's
life to live by . . .

bitterly

woman's either!

76

Herakles: A life is inconceivable without the silence
              answering somehow!

              *He hurls himself against the enormous door, strug-
              gling with it, all his strength.*

Megara: *up the steps*

                                  No! Come with me!
              Come with me! Oh, come away!
              We need the edge of ignorance to live by,
              the little, ignorant unknown of time
              beyond us in the dark that could be anything . . .

She drags at him.

              Even the worst, inevitable certainty
              cannot be certain till we know.

He shakes her off.

              Hide from me, Sun, what comes to pass
              beyond these moments on this grass . . .

              beyond this warmth against these bones . . .

              against these bones . . .

The Guide: He wants his
              promise, lady.

          insolently

                  You remember!

77

*The huge door buckles, gives, grinds open: on a golden tripod
in a bride's dress, an aged woman blinking at the light.*

Little Hodd: She's the one!
                    Is she the one?
            He puts his voice in her mouth, you said,
            like a bell's tongue in a bell, you said —
            the god does — and she tells, she tells . . .

Miss Parfit: Flesh to tell and god for tongue:
            mortal by immortal rung . . .
            that's how it was in the world once.

Mrs. Hoadley: That's how it always has been — poor
            body jangling to the word of god
            like a cracked bell to an iron hammer.
            Either the words are too hard for the mouth
            or the mouth's too weak for the words: it stam-
                   mers.

Herakles:

To Xenoclea: she shades her eyes, staring at him.

            You know me.

Silence.

            You know me, don't you?

Xenoclea: *old woman's cracked voice*

            Herakles . . .

Her voice breaks: half man's, half woman's.

Herakles!
        Where the smouldering sun
set the heaped-up sky on fire . . .

The Guide: So! So he's there after all, is he?
           He might have made a signal somehow . . .

Herakles: *reverently*

        It's a long time back since you and I . . .

Silence: he waits.

        You saw it, didn't you? You see everything.

Silence: his voice rising

        Speak to me, Lord God Apollo!

He lunges forward.

Megara: Oh no! Don't touch her!

The Guide: Aie! Herakles!

Megara: Oh, come down! Come down! Come down!

Herakles: I've done my part, God Apollo!

        Persist against impossible, unequal odds,
        set the world straight, staunch the horror,
        slaughter the enemies and then? . . . and then?

79

Who told me what would happen then?
Who told me that, Apollo? You!

Silence: he is raging

A short life and shit to your knees! —
that's what the world was once. Now look at it!

The Guide: Look at it! Look at it, Apollo!
A clean, well-lighted reasonable universe
where happiness is possible at last!

Herakles: Answer me, Lord God Apollo!

Xenoclea: *her body convulsed: a great man's voice twisting her*
mouth

I have no oracle for such as you.

Herakles: *violently*

You have no oracle for me! For *me!*
Break your fingers on the bucking oar!
Spend your proud, improvident, last, gasping
heartful of exhausted blood
beating the seas back! Reach your journey!
Claim the promise you were promised some-
    where
far off in the morning long ago and
what's the answer? There is no answer.
By God! . . .

He seizes the golden tripod, the women screaming.

I'll answer it myself!

He pitches Xenoclea down the steps, lifts the tripod toward the sun.

The Guide: Herakles! Herakles!

Nothing happens. The sun blazes. Silence. Xenoclea stirs, huddles on the stone, looks up at him, the golden tripod in his hand like a club.

Xenoclea: *the old woman's voice*

Aie, Herakles . . .

she peers at him

Not young . . .
                   not what you used to be . . .

all those deeds of yours, those doings,
unnatural animals, half man, half beast . . .

men like beasts but men . . .
                   Don't tell me!
It's all one like the salt in the sea . . .

wandering

Everything else will wash away
but the salt stays in the sea . . .
                   it stays . . .

that's where we end . . .
with the salt in the sea . . .

The Guide: He's slaughtered the enemies, Xenoclea, all the
enemies. Now the promises come true.

Xenoclea: I know . . .
I've heard about it . . .
Hero!
Everything unnatural, inhuman,
dead in the suds at the sea's edge
or up in a hole in the hills or somewhere . . .

all but one.

The Guide: Not one. Not one.
There's not a horror anywhere . . .

Xenoclea: . . . but one.

Herakles: What one?

Xenoclea: *cowering*

The last unconquerable horror!

Little Hodd: What are you frightened of, Xenoclea?

Xenoclea: The god.

staring at Herakles

Aren't you?

82

looking from one to another

                             Aren't any of you?

Miss Parfit: Poor thing! Poor thing!
                  She's strayed: she's off in the barley somewhere.

Xenoclea: The god!

     terrified; lost in herself

            You feel him breathing in you,
    drawing breath in you to speak
    the way the wind draws breath among
    exhausted trees to bring the gale back . . .

     screaming

           Aie! when it comes!
                      When it comes!
                             When it comes!
    The will goes over the won't like a stallion
    over a precipice — right off —
    clean into nothing at all with a clatter of
    hovering hooves and it falls . . .
                          befalls . . .

Silence.

    I'm not mad whatever they've said to you . . .
    letting the lizards run over my hands . . .

    over my hands . . .

my hands . . .

Silence.

                                    There is blood on your
                hands, Herakles.

Herakles: My enemies'.

Xenoclea: What enemies?

Megara: *desperately*

                How can he tell you in a world like this one —
                always the bewildered light,
                the altering sky, the clouds changing
                every which way with the wind, with night's
                dissolving distances?
                                        There's only
                one thing, certain in this world, this wild,
                this wilderness, this shine and shadow . . .

                evil is under the bright air.

Xenoclea: What enemies, Herakles?

Herakles: Apollo knows! . . .
                blow by blow, year after year of it,
                wherever the grasses stirred, the terror
                startled from the tossing grass . . .

Xenoclea: The blood . . .
                        It is your blood, Herakles.

Herakles: Mine!
            I haven't a scratch. They never touched me.

Xenoclea: No, they never touched you, Herakles . . .

        She is wandering.

            Not mad whatever they said to you . . .

            letting the lizards run over my hands . . .

Silence.

            How many children have you, Herakles?

Megara: No! No! No! No!

Herakles: Seven sons.

Xenoclea: Whose blood have they, Herakles?

Herakles: Whose do you think?
                            You think that *she* —
            that kind of woman?
                            Besides they look like me —
            follow me round like colts after cabbages . . .

            used to . . .
                        morning noon and night.

Xenoclea: Think of them, Herakles. Try to think of them.

Herakles: When I forget my seven sons!

                            85

Mrs. Hoadley: Terror touches me . . .
                                    cold finger . . .

Xenoclea: Try to remember them — each one.

The Guide: Shadow of what cloud goes over
              cloudless . . .

Megara: Oh, my sons! My sons!

Xenoclea: It all comes true when you remember.

Silence.

              Let your mind remember, Herakles:
              it's trying to remember. Let it!
              Don't be afraid.

Herakles: There's not a creature
              dead or living I'm afraid of.

Xenoclea: So! Go back to them, Herakles.

Herakles: Back
              where?

Xenoclea: You'll know.

Heracles: Beside the gate there . . .

Xenoclea: Look at them, Herakles!

86

Herakles: They've fallen:
              how can I face them when they've fallen?

Xenoclea: Lift their heads!
                              Lift their heads!
              Lift their bloody heads!

Herakles: No!

Xenoclea: You are remembering, Herakles. Look at them!

Herakles: Take them away!

Xenoclea: I cannot take them . . .

      gently: rising from the steps

      I cannot see them, Herakles.

She comes down, wanders off among the stones, vanishes.

Megara: No, but
              we can! W*e* can!
                      Nothing is blind to us
      born of the world as we are — odor of
      earth's cold or kindness — smoke
      blown from a roof in the rain or the stain of
      blood in the dust. We see — we learn to:
      even death we learn to see.

Herakles: The oracle has betrayed me!

He flings himself onto the tripod: his face in his hands.

87

Megara: No,
            the oracle has not betrayed you.
            You wanted to be god. You are.

Mrs. Hoadley: Have pity on yourself.

Herakles: Pity!
            Roll in pity for myself like dogs in
            carrion!
                        A man is made for anger isn't he? —
            to stand up, strike back,
            fight in the snow-fall in the tricks of light
            in the wild air — ills encountered
            everywhere that ills befall,
            fear befalls . . .

Megara: But not to kill as
            god kills — as the will of god.
            Oh no! It isn't death that's horrible.
            Death is everywhere, the winter
            gentle with it with the brittle leaves
            like fragile bones . . .
                                cold, quiet embers.

            What's horrible is the will of god —
            the pure, indifferent, effortless, cold will
            that kills because it can . . .

                                destroys as
            seas do, shattering, because they can . . .

            as gales because they can among the villages.

Nothing, neither love nor trust
nor happiness matters to the will of god:
it *can* and down the city tumbles . . .

down the children in the bloody dust.

Nothing is terrible as the will of god
that can and can and can . . .

He lifts his face from his hands, sits staring at the sun.

                    Listen to me!
Listen, Herakles, in that blind light
where you see everything and are alone,
miserable . . .

She starts up the steps.

           I do not ask you to return to me . . .
not to me . . .

Another step.

           You do not understand it.
You have swept the world, lit the dark,
mastered the horrors and are god and
miserable . . .

Another step

           There is only one way back —
bury our sons . . .
           help me bury them.

89

No one else can do it for us:
the god cannot do it.
Only human
hands can bury what we have to bury . . .

she has come to the open door

Afterward we'll wash our hands
together on the stones there by the water . . .

she picks up his hands in hers.

our unhappy
hands . . .

He does not speak or move

Hurt heals. That's what the sea says.
The god cannot hear it but we hear it.

Herakles: *violently: his face blazing in the sun*

By god, I'll give the oracles myself.
I'll see and say and say and say . . .

a shout

I'll answer it!

*Megara turns, pulls her shawl over her head, descends the steps,
goes off, goes out. The Guide hesitates, pulls his cap over his
eyes, follows her. The door swings shut, a heavy clang that
echoes once and again and again and faster and fading and gone.*

Mrs. Hoadley: Oh, release me from this broken story,
this myth remembered by a mouth of stone
among the stone mouths of the ruined fountain!
Let me go back to my life wherever my
life was or is or will be waiting
wandering up and down from the one
morning to the other morning,
from the one despair to the next, from the
hope in
this day to the hope in that one . . .

Oh, release me from this mortal story!

She starts out, Miss Parfit behind her. Little Hodd runs up the steps, touches the enormous door. It opens to her hand. There is nothing — only the sky blue with light. A sound of goatbells far off as at the beginning. Little Hodd runs down, follows the others.